A DROP O' WINE

A DROP O' WINE
MOLLIE HARRIS

ILLUSTRATED BY
LOUIS MACKAY

CHATTO & WINDUS

THE HOGARTH PRESS
LONDON

Published in 1983 by
Chatto & Windus · The Hogarth Press
40 William IV Street
London WC2N 4DF

Second impression 1986

British Library Cataloguing in Publication Data
Harris, Mollie
A drop o'wine
1. Wine and wine making—Amateurs' manuals
I. Title
641.8'72   TP548.2
ISBN 0 7011 2690 6

Printed in Great Britain by
Redwood Burn Limited, Trowbridge, Wiltshire

CONTENTS

I would like to thank all my friends and acquaintances, past and present, who have so readily given me their own particular recipes for wine, which have helped to make this book possible.

MOLLIE HARRIS

To my friend Petra Lewis whose idea it was
I should write this book

FOREWORD

Wine-making can be inexpensive and *very* simple. If you need to go in for complicated and scientific processes then this is no book for you. But I can assure you that it is possible for the beginner to produce good wines with minimum equipment and a little patience, and at half the cost of shop wines. It need not be time-consuming either – unless, of course, you want it to be. But the pleasure, pride and sense of achievement when you open that very first bottle is worth any effort involved. Then there are the friendships that wine-making can bring, competitions to enter, wine-tasting sessions in friends' homes, swapping hints and recipes and, above all, a wonderful feeling of satisfaction from the realisation that you have produced a brain-tickling wine from something you may well have thought to be a useless weed.

Blackberry wine is one of the loveliest I produce; and what could be better than to sally forth on a balmy autumn day, when dew-wet cobwebs hang like jewels on every branch and twig, to gather succulent blackberries? For the trip you need to be wearing sensible shoes and slacks, and go armed with a nice wicker basket and a walking stick to drag down the berries that seem almost out of reach. Pick the best of the fruit – you really don't want overripe ones. If you gather yours from by the roadside, a quick wipe in a clean tea-towel should remove the dust and dirt: but try *not* to gather fruit or flowers from a busy roadside.

Keep your eyes open as you travel round, especially in the

early spring, and note where the snowy white blackthorn blossom blooms – come late-September, early-October, there should be lots of lovely sharp blue-black sloe berries on the branches. Sloe wine is lovely, and sloe gin even better. Elderberries are easy to spot and very prolific, and grow almost everywhere in the autumn. And a sharp eye can notice where wild crab-apples hang like small lanterns on leafless trees in late autumn, and gorse a-blooming on common ground. Throughout the year look out for stinging nettles, rose hips, the blossom and the leaves of the may bush. Even young oak and walnut leaves can be used for wine-making, while coltsfoot flowers make an excellent drink (for years in my extreme youth I was afraid to pick them – they were nicknamed 'pee the bed', and were supposed to make you do just that). Dandelions, of course, produce one of the nicest of wines, and my gramp swore by agrimony wine – agrimony is a tall yellow wild flower – for his rheumatics.

Then there are all the garden fruit and vegetables, almost all of which can be used in wine-making.

So what about it? Why not have a go? Soon you will be producing brain-tickling wine along with the rest of us.

There are two reasons for drinking; one is, when you are thirsty; the other when you are not thirsty, to prevent it.

THOMAS LOVE PEACOCK 1785–1866

INTRODUCTION

A glance at the index will, I hope both refresh half-forgotten country memories and whet the taste of townsfolk, so that the reader may be encouraged to start to make their own wines from damsons and dandelions, elderflowers and elderberries, parsnips and parsley, and many, many other things. The fields and hedgerows and, indeed, most gardens make a great contribution to our cellars in this way. But if you haven't a garden or don't live in the country, there are still fruits and vegetables that can be bought in the shops which can be made into wine. Of course, this makes it a bit more expensive to make but, even so, a great deal cheaper than 'boughten' wine.

There's nothing new under the sun about making home-made wine, for according to tradition it was Noah who planted the first vineyard, and there's a most beautiful fifteenth-century illuminated manuscript which depicts Noah in his vineyard along with members of the family, gathering and pressing the grapes. He was a very wise man to have had the good sense to save a pair of each species of animal, and also to have concocted one of man's greatest blessings, the making of wine: a method which has altered little over the centuries, except that we don't tread our ingredients. In Genesis we read that 'Noah drank of the wine and was drunken' – but then perhaps Noah, like my grandparents, drank it, as they said, 'mostly for medicinal reasons'.

Well, if it was Noah that started the craze for home-made wine making, others were quick to follow, and since then princes and peasants, monks and monarchs, Romans and robbers, wives and witches, have made their own wines. The ancient Greeks were great wine-makers: so too were the Egyptians – we know by looking at tomb paintings that wine was drunk by them some 4,000 years ago.

The Elizabethans considered wine to be part of their medicinal necessities – making much use of herbs and flowers for their favourite drinks and cures. Jane Austen, Mrs Gaskell and George Eliot all came from families that went in for home-made wine-making. And Shakespeare himself wrote:

> With thy grapes our hairs be crowned,
> Cup us till the world goes round
> Cup us till the world goes round.

But my initiation into wine drinking – for you must taste the 'drink of the gods' before you get the urge to make some for yourself – started when I was quite young, during my school summer holidays, when I visited my grandparents in the beautiful village of Sherbourne, in the Cotswolds. I can truly say that it was they who gave me a liking for it – not that, I must add, they gave me glasses of the stuff, which in those far-off days was not drunk solely for pleasure, but more often for genuinely medicinal reasons. A visit from the doctor and any medicine provided by him had to be paid for in those days, so self-heal was very much in evidence.

And to 'take a drop o wine' could do a body a power of good – parsley for the bladder and kidneys and to enrich the blood, dandelion as a splendid tonic and for a sluggish liver: the list was endless. Visitors and neighbours too were asked 'to take a drop o wine' – there was little else that anyone could afford to offer in the way of hospitality in those hard-up times.

But my first taste of those summer wines was when my gran gave me a few winey raisins on a saucer – some that she had strained from her dandelion wine as she bottled it off, for lots of people did, and still do, add a handful of raisins in to give it flavour and add a little sweetness. Sitting up at her kitchen table, snowy white with years of scrubbing, I'd watch her busy with her housework while I sucked and savoured the summer sweetness from those plump, fat raisins – and sometimes, when she had given me rather a lot, I'd fall off to sleep, my head dropping onto the table, only to wake up later with a bit of a headache and a stiff neck. One of my gran's own sayings about her wine was 'keep it warm while it's working, and cool when it's clearing'. I've always remembered that and stuck to it.

After my gran died I used to stay in the same village with an uncle and aunt who were also great wine-makers. They had a farm and were up early every morning milking the cows and doing manual farmwork, and they were always ready for their dinner at twelve o'clock. As soon as the pudding had been eaten my aunt would get up, go to a small cupboard by the side of the fireplace, and bring out a large jug of wine and a couple of glasses. She and uncle would 'take a drop o wine', and after the second glass they would promptly fall asleep for about twenty minutes. As a child twenty minutes of trying to keep still and quiet seemed a lifetime, and I used to fidget and wake them up. Then Auntie had a great idea: why not give the child a drop, she suggested. So that was it – after I'd scoffed mine I fell off to sleep as well.

My aunt told me that they would sometimes mull wine during the Cotswold winters. Elderberry is the best for mulling: they would thrust a red-hot poker into a jug of two-year-old elderberry, then, warmed and wined, it was off to bed to sleep soundly till 'twas time to get up for milking again. And over the years the wine-making of my gran, auntie and mother rubbed off onto me. Now I make several lots throughout the year. It's a very satisfying sight to see a rack of sparkling wines and several stone casks of the stuff maturing in my larder.

STARTING OUT

There is no need for a lot of elaborate and expensive equipment – after all, how did our grandmothers and mothers manage to produce good drinkable wines? Most of the things you need you probably already have in your kitchen.

For all *my* wine-making, I use an earthenware pan – it was my gran's, and very useful it is too – but a large white plastic bucket or a large bowl will do just as well. Then you'll need a funnel, most probably of plastic. Never use anything tinny or iron-based as an unpleasant flavour can be imparted into the wines; aluminium and glass are all right, however. And you will need a large jug, say a quart one, and muslin for straining the wine – I use a fine old nylon net curtain which answers the purpose beautifully.

My only modern investment is a demijohn. For years and years I never bothered with one, but they are useful during fermentation, which is the next stage of wine-making. My daughter-in-law presented me with mine – she said that she was fed up with the sound of gunfire coming from my larder. You see, if you put wine straight into bottles the corks blow out – and she reckoned that to sit in our cottage was like being at the Battle of Waterloo. So she presented me with a demijohn and an air lock, and since then I have wondered how on earth I managed all those years without one. Now I own several.

You will also need a bung and an airlock which are fitted into the demijohn, a wooden spoon, a packet of paper filters, a small piece of plastic tubing to syphon the wine from the

demijohn (not absolutely essential), a few campden tablets and, later on, some bottles complete with corks – and, *if* you can get hold of one, a good old-fashioned stone cask to store your wine in, before bottling it off.

Once you start making wine, think how often you will be able to enjoy the fruits of your labours – not only you, but your friends too. And there is a lot to be said for swapping tips and ideas over a glass of wine.

After you've made your first gallon of wine, don't just sit back waiting until it's fit to drink, but set about making different types, so that by the time the first lot is ready you will have a steady supply to follow.

To make all wine, the method is very much the same. Yeast and sugar are added to a mixture of juice and water: sometimes the water used is cold and poured over the main ingredients, sometimes boiling water is called for, and sometimes the ingredients are boiled. The enzyme in the yeast works the sugar and the yeast begins to breed, producing millions of little cells which live on the sugar, gradually turning your wine into alcohol and gas – the bubbles that are given off during the fermentation period.

Try to keep your working wine in a temperature of 65° F – that's easy to do in the summertime, but watch your winter wines that they don't get cold. Friends of mine keep theirs in the airing cupboard during the really cold weather.

The sweetness or dryness of wine depends on the amount of sugar you use in each batch: $2\frac{1}{2}$ lb of sugar to each gallon of juice will produce a dry or medium-dry wine, while $3\frac{1}{2}$–4 lb will give you a lovely sweet wine. Always use granulated sugar unless otherwise stated. Should you get one that turns out too dry, or even one that turns out too sweet, not to worry – 'come drinking time', and you can always blend them with others to the dryness or sweetness that suits your palate.

For years I used ordinary solid baker's yeast which I bought from our local baker, an ounce at a time, just when I needed it. But I find that ordinary packets of bread yeast serve the same purpose, although I know that not everyone agrees with this method. If you *must* buy special yeast, do so by all means, but I never do.

[17]

Soon after the yeast has been added, you will notice that an inch or two of froth will form on the top, which means that the wine is working well.

Always keep your wines covered with a thick cloth in the early stages (before they go into the demijohn) otherwise you might be plagued with wine flies, which seem to be able to detect homemade wine a mile off (although my brother, who once worked for a wine merchant, said that they had to watch out for them when they were bottling off some of their good wines). They are very small blackish-brown flies, and if they get into your wine they can quite easily turn a good wine sharp and sour, like vinegar – indeed some folks call them vinegar flies. You will also notice them flying around when you are decanting wine for drinking purposes.

Once your wine is made and you have funnelled the strained wine into your demijohn, which you should always fill – you can top it up with a little water if necessary. Fix in your bung and an airlock; the air-lock should have a little water in it. Stand the demijohn on a tray and then place it in a fairly warm room – a kitchen is ideal.

After a little while you will notice that the water in the air lock will, quite regularly, omit a bubble, which means that your wine is working well. Leave it in the demijohn till this working has ceased – some wines take longer than others – and then bottle off, or put into a cask and leave to mature. Once you think that the wine is drinkable, the best thing to do is to decant it. Have some clean bottles ready, along with a funnel and some wine filter papers. Line the funnel with a filter paper and put it in the top of an empty bottle. Now pour or syphon the wine from the demijohn through the funnel and into the clean bottle: gradually it will drip through the filter, clearing it as it does so. Occasionally you will have to renew the wine paper when it becomes discoloured or the wine doesn't seem to be dripping through. This is a slow job and can be fixed in between other jobs about the house. If, when you have decanted all the wine, it is not quite clear, leave it in the bottles for another few weeks, after which you may have to decant it again.

If you store your wine in a cask rather than in bottles, you must be very careful when you come to decant it. There is bound to be some sediment at the bottom and you really don't want to keep this. If you just tip the cask up to get the wine out, the sediment will cloud all the wine. The best thing to do is to syphon off the wine from the sediment. For this you will need a piece of clean rubber or plastic tubing a quarter or half an inch in diameter. I simply suck mine up through the tube to get it started, but you can buy a special syphon tube or syphon pump if you wish. Discard all sediment.

To make sure that your containers are clean and free from any bacteria sterilize them, either with ordinary washing soda, using 4 oz to a gallon of boiling water, or crush six campden tablets in a pint of water (this mixture can be used again and again before you discard it).

Once a bottle of home-made wine has been opened it will keep indefinitely, unlike boughten wines. And all wines improve with keeping. Always be sure that your wine is *cool*, but not *cold*, before adding the yeast.

PROBLEMS AND CURES

It doesn't matter how good a wine-maker you are or how many years you have been at it, just occasionally one batch might not turn out as good as you expected it to. Provided you follow the instructions and recipes properly and your equipment has all been sterilised, all should be well. So what can go wrong?

LOSS OF COLOUR

Your beetroot, blackberry, sloe and elderberry should range in colour from red to burgundy. But if you leave it in a strong light too long the wine might lose some of the attractive colour. Keep fermenting wines away from direct strong sunlight. If you must put it in a sunny window, then wrap several thicknesses of brown paper round the demijohn.

WINE TURNING INTO VINEGAR

This sometimes happens if you have not completely filled your jar (or whatever you keep your wine in after fermentation has stopped), or if the wine is kept in too damp and cold a place. A wise wine-maker should not run this risk. If it does occur, try crushing a campden tablet and add it to the jar, and leave for a couple of days. If this doesn't do the trick then it's probably too late to save the wine, but at least you will have a good supply of wine vinegar.

THINNESS

If your wine tastes thin and weak, then you haven't used enough fruit or vegetables – at least, not as much as the recipe states. Sometimes when the recipe says (e.g.) 3 lb of plums you may well weigh them stones and all – but after you have de-stoned them the end product will *not* be 3 lb. If you think your wine is thin, the best thing is to blend it with a thick one like, say, elderberry.

CLOUDINESS

Some wines in the early stage, and for no reason at all, can look like pea-soup, cloudy and awful to look at, and not all that nice to taste. The thing to do is bottle it off, store it away and forget about it for a year or longer. You will then find that most of the wrongs have been put right and you have bottles of clear, pleasant-tasting wine. Once I made some rose petal wine and it turned out so dry that no one wanted it. So I stored it away and forgot about it. Four years later I remembered it, fetched it out and by then somehow it had lost a deal of its dryness, and I was left with some *very* nice wine. But afterwards when I was telling the tale to a very experienced winemaker he said, 'All you needed to do was to add half an ounce of glycerine to each pint of wine.'

Don't be put off with the things that *can* go wrong: follow the instructions properly, and there is very little that time and common sense won't put right.

HANDY MEASUREMENTS

If the following are required for ONE GALLON	the working equivalent for FIVE LITRES will be
1 lb	500 g
2 lb	1000 g or 1 kilo
½ lb	250 g
¼ lb	125 g
2 oz	60 g
1 oz	30 g
½ oz	15 g
4 pints	2.5 litres
2 pints	1.25 litres
1 pint	600 ml
1 fluid oz	30 ml
½ fluid oz	15 ml

1 gallon equals 4.55 litres
2.2 lb equals 1 kilo

HOME-MADE WINES

AGRIMONY WINE

You can use this wild flower either fresh or dried. If you are using fresh agrimony the time to make this wine is from June till August. If you dry it, then you can make it at your leisure.

Some people may not know what it looks like. Found by the roadside or in grass fields, it grows up to nearly two feet high, and has little yellow flowers all the way up the stem. What you need is

A GOOD BUNCH OF AGRIMONY, FLOWERS, LEAVES
AND STALKS (*as much as you can hold in your hand*),
3 LEMONS, 4 ORANGES, 3 OZ ROOT GINGER,
2 GALLONS WATER, 6½ lb SUGAR, WHITE OR
DEMERARA, ½ OZ YEAST

Bruise the ginger and put it along with the bunch of agrimony into a large saucepan. Add half the water and boil up together until the water has changed colour to amber. Then add the rest of the water and bring to the boil again. Then tip in the sugar and thinly sliced lemons and oranges, and sprinkle on the yeast. Cover with a cloth and leave for four days. Strain, transfer the wine to your demijohn, and proceed as on page 18.

This wine is very good for rheumatism and severe colds, and can be drunk six months after making. It also makes a nice semi-sweet dinner wine.

APPLE WINE

Apple wine can be made from late August until early October; and for it you will need

8 lb WINDFALL APPLES, COOKERS OR EATERS
I GALLON WATER, SUGAR, ½ OZ YEAST

Cut the apples up into small pieces; don't peel them, but cut out any bad bits. Put them into your bucket or large bowl, pour the water, cold, over them, sprinkle on the yeast. Cover with a cloth, and leave for four days. Stir vigorously two or three times a day. After the fourth day strain through your muslin or fine curtain, squeezing well to get out all the juice. Tip the juice back into your bucket, and add three pounds of sugar to every gallon of liquid. Cover well with a thick cloth, and leave in a warmish place – the kitchen will do. Take a peep after a few hours to see if it's working well. You can tell if it is, for it should have an inch or two of froth on the top. This applies to *all* wines after the yeast has been added. Leave in the bucket for about a week. Strain again, tip it into your demijohn, and proceed as on page 18.

Watch this wine, as it is supposed to have aphrodisiac qualities. A sweet delicate wine, it will be drinkable after four months.

APRICOT AND RAISIN WINE

This wine can be made at any time throughout the year.

2 lb DRIED APRICOTS, 1 lb RAISINS (*chopped*),
1 GALLON WATER, 2½ TO 3 lb SUGAR, *depending on how
sweet* you *want it,* ½ OZ YEAST

Chop up the apricots quite small and soak overnight in cold
water, just enough to cover the fruit. Next day tip this into
your bucket or bowl, and pour over it a gallon of boiling water.
Cover with a thick cloth and leave for three days. Strain off the
liquid and tip this back into the bucket. Add the sugar and
chopped raisins, stirring with a wooden spoon till all has dissolved. Sprinkle the yeast on top, cover and leave for a week.
Strain into the demijohn, and proceed as on page 18. This
makes a delightful sweet wine, drinkable within five months.

APRICOT WINE FROM
FRESH FRUIT

Here is one for fresh apricots – if you ever have enough to spare to make into a wine that is absolutely delicious.

6 lb FRESH APRICOTS, 1 GALLON BOILING WATER,
3 lb SUGAR, ½ oz YEAST

Place the apricots in your bucket and with both hands squeeze the fruit until it is quite pulpy, removing the stones at the same time. Pour over the boiling water. Cover and leave in a warm place for a couple of days. Strain, and tip back into your bucket. Add the sugar, stir well, then add the yeast. Cover and leave for a further four days. Strain again, tip it all into your demijohn, and proceed as on page 18.

This is a beautiful golden-coloured wine with a delicate bouquet, and will be drinkable after six months.

BARLEY WINE

This is best made in February or March.

   1 lb OLD POTATOES, 1 lb WASHED RAISINS,
   3 lb DEMERARA SUGAR, 1 lb BARLEY (*begged from a farmer*), ½ OZ YEAST, 1 GALLON WATER

Scrub the potatoes, cut them up quite small, and put them into your wine-making container. Add the sugar. Then add barley and raisins, which I put through a very coarse mincer. (An old recipe I once used said crush your barley: I did so and it shot all over the kitchen, so I find that mincing the barley and raisins together is the best plan.) Add the gallon of boiling water and stir until you feel all the sugar has dissolved. When the wine is cool, add a half ounce of yeast. Cover very closely for three or four days. Then strain, put into your demijohn and fix the airlock. Proceed as on page 18. Usually quite a lot of deposit forms in your jar after a few days, in which case syphon the wine off into another demijohn, fix the airlock and leave it to get on with the fermenting, which will take four or five weeks. Bottle off when all movement has stopped.

If left to mature for a couple of years, this wine tastes almost like whisky – but it can be drunk within six months. Good for sufferers from bronchitis and asthma.

BEETROOT WINE

This is best made in December or January.

4 lb BEETROOT *or* 2 lb BEETROOT AND 2 lb PARSNIPS,
1 GALLON WATER, 3 lb DEMERARA SUGAR, 2 LEMONS,
½ OZ ROOT GINGER, 4 CLOVES, ½ OZ YEAST
1 WINEGLASS BRANDY (*optional*)

Scrub the beetroots clean and cut them up into small pieces. Place in a saucepan with the ginger and cloves, and cover with the water. Cook until tender but not mushy. Strain off the liquid into a large bowl or bucket. Add the sugar and the lemon juice and stir till all the sugar has dissolved. Add the yeast when the liquid is cool. Cover with a cloth and leave for four days. Strain through muslin and pour into demijohn: then proceed as on page 18. Keep the wine out of strong sunlight as it will take the colour out of it – it's a good idea to wrap your demijohn round with brown paper. After it has stopped working strain off your wine into jars, bottles or a cask.

Beetroot wine is especially good for anaemia.

This wine is much better if kept a year or more – it improves a great deal with age. And is even better if a wine glass of brandy is added just before bottling it off (this will produce a full-bodied wine).

A different tasting wine, drier and more potent, can be made by using 2 lb of beetroot and 2 lb of parsnips in place of the 4 lb of beetroot. Prepare the parsnips in the same way as the beetroot.

BLACKBERRY WINE

You can make this wine from mid-August till mid-October.
It is one of my favourites, and so simple to make. You will
need

4 lb RIPE BLACKBERRIES, 1 GALLON WATER,
3 lb SUGAR (*or* 2¼ *lb for a drier wine*), 1 OZ YEAST,
6 OZ RAISINS (*for a sweeter wine*)

Roll the berries very gently in a tea towel to remove the dust,
but don't wash them on any account. Place them in a large
bowl or bucket and pour over them a gallon of boiling water.
Cover with a cloth and leave for three days, stirring a couple
of times each day. Strain the liquid on to the sugar and stir
well till you feel it has all dissolved. Leave for half an hour, and
then add the yeast and cover closely. Leave in the container
for a further six days. Then strain, put into the demijohn, and
proceed as on page 18.

It should be ready to drink when six months old. Should
you need a really sweet wine to serve with your sweet, add
six ounces of raisins when you add the boiling water. For a
specially dry wine only use 2¼ lb of sugar and *no* raisins.

Only pick blackberries from brambles that are too high for
a dog to cock his leg on. And never pick them after 12 October,
for after that date *the devil spits on them.*

BLACKCURRANT WINE

The time to make this wine with fresh fruit is July and August. However, blackcurrants can be frozen successfully, in which case you can make it at your leisure.

This wine is made a little differently from most, and for it you need

3 lb BLACKCURRANTS, 3½ lb SUGAR, 1 GALLON WATER,
½ OZ YEAST

Remove the stalks from the fruit and roll it in a clean tea towel. Place the blackcurrants in a large bowl or bucket. Boil the sugar and water up together and pour at once over the fruit. Leave until cool, but not cold, before sprinkling on the yeast. Cover closely and keep in a fairly warm place for five or six days. Strain, put in to demijohn, and continue as on page 18.

Blackcurrant wine is especially good for colds and coughs. Warm gently, almost to boiling point, and drink it hot – preferably in bed. It tastes deliciously of blackcurrants, is lovely served with your sweet, and is drinkable after six months.

Redcurrant wine can be made up in the same way, using the same method and quantities. It is a very different tasting wine, sweeter and more delicate, and paler in colour. Drinkable after five months.

BRAMBLE TIP WINE

Look out for the new leaf growth on the blackberry brambles
in April and May, for this wine is best made in the spring when
the young bramble shoots are tender. Pinch them off the top of
the stalks with your finger and thumb – there shouldn't be too
many thorns early in the year.

4 lb BRAMBLE OR BLACKBERRY SHOOTS,
1 lb RAISINS, 1 GALLON WATER, 1 LEMON,
2½ lb SUGAR, ½ OZ YEAST

Chop up the tips and then boil them up in the gallon of water
for about half an hour. Strain off into a large bowl or bucket.
Add the chopped raisins, sugar, and grated lemon rind and
juice. Stir, then leave to get cool before adding the yeast. Cover
closely and leave for at least five days before straining into the
demijohn: then proceed as on page 18.

This will make a medium dry wine, drinkable within six
months.

BROAD BEAN WINE

At some time or other most gardeners end up with a quantity of broad beans – probably in excess of those needed for seed. A delightful dry wine can be made from them, and what you will need is

4 lb OLD BROAD BEANS (*after they have been shelled*),
4 oz SULTANAS, I LEMON, I GALLON WATER,
3 lb SUGAR, ½ oz YEAST

Shell the beans and simmer them in the water for about an hour. Strain the liquor off into a large bowl or bucket and add the chopped sultanas, lemon juice and sugar. Stir well until the sugar has dissolved. Add the yeast when the wine is cool but not cold. Cover with a thick cloth and leave for six days. Strain into your demijohn, fix the airlock, then proceed as on page 18.

This makes a nice amber-coloured dry wine; it can be drunk when six months old but is best left for a year.

CARROT WINE

Use old carrots for this wine – a good time to make it is February or March when they are really mature.

4 lb CARROTS (*without the green tops*), 4 lb DEMERARA SUGAR, 1 GALLON WATER, THE JUICE OF TWO GRAPEFRUITS AND TWO ORANGES, 1 OZ ROOT GINGER, 1 OZ YEAST

Scrub the carrots but don't peel them. Slice them quite thinly and put them into a large saucepan. Add the water and crushed ginger and boil until the carrots are *quite* tender. Strain the liquid onto the sugar and stir well: then leave to cool. Add the fruit juices and the yeast. Cover with a cloth and leave for a week. Then strain off into your demijohn; fix the airlock then proceed as on page 18.

Carrot wine is reputed to be very good for gout sufferers, but also makes an excellent wine to serve with your main meal. It is best left for ten months before drinking.

CHERRY WINE

Made when cherries are at their best, this will produce a lovely rich fruity wine.

1 QUART BLACK CHERRIES, 4 lb SUGAR, 3 QUARTS
COLD WATER, 1 QUART PALE ALE, A SPRINKLING
OF YEAST

Measure the cherries in a jug, prick each one with a needle. Tip all the ingredients into your bowl or bucket, stir well and cover with a thick cloth. Stand in a warm room for about two weeks, then strain the wine into your demijohn, fix the airlock and continue as on page 18.

Cherry wine improves with keeping, so try not to use for a year. The strained cherries make quite a nice pie filling.

❧ HEARD IN THE VILLAGE STREET: '*My old man 'ull drink home-made wine till the cows come home, he can drink pints and that don't affect him at all, 'tis like puttin' a hot bread poultice on a wooden leg.*'

COLTSFOOT WINE

Coltsfoot flowers are among the first to show up on the road-side verges in late February or early March. They are bright yellow, and usually grow in large clumps. You will need

1 GALLON COLTSFOOT FLOWERS, 3½ lb SUGAR,
2 ORANGES AND 2 LEMONS, 1 GALLON WATER,
½ OZ YEAST

Gather the coltsfoot flowers on a fine day, cut the heads off as clear of as much green as possible, and place in a large container. Boil up the water and sugar together for a few moments, and pour over the flowers. Add the juice and rinds of the fruits and stir well. When the liquid is cool add the yeast and cover closely, and leave for five or six days. Strain into your demijohn and proceed as on page 18.

Coltsfoot flowers make a lovely amber-coloured semi-sweet wine, something like dandelion wine, which is drinkable after six months.

CRAB-APPLE WINE

This delicious and colourful country wine is best made in early October. Choose the rosiest crab-apples you can find.

3 lb CRAB-APPLES, 3 lb DEMERARA SUGAR,
1 GALLON WATER, 1 OZ YEAST

Slice each crab-apple in two, pour over the boiling water and leave in a covered bucket for a week. Strain off the liquor onto the demerara sugar. Stir well when cool. Add the yeast, cover closely and leave for six days before turning all into your demijohn and proceeding as on page 18.

Crab-apple wine is best if kept for at least a year.

🌱 *One day I went to see an old gamekeeper friend of mine and his wife, and they invited me into their warm cosy kitchen. I could see the old brick-built washing copper in the corner of the room, but guessed that it was no longer used for that. The little iron door at the bottom through which countless housewives had pushed wood and coal to boil up their washing in the old days was black and shiny, and the wooden lid was varnished and polished. Catching my glance the gamekeeper said, 'Ah, I'll bet you dunt knaw what we keeps in thear.' Then he lifted the lid, and the inside was filled with bottles of home-made wine – which of course we sampled!*

DAMSON WINE

This is best made in late August or September.

4 lb DAMSONS (*ripe but firm*), 1 GALLON WATER,
3 lb SUGAR, ½ OZ YEAST, 1 WINEGLASSFUL OF BRANDY

Wipe the damsons clean, take off any stalks, and place the unstoned fruit in your container. Pour a gallon of boiling water over the fruit and bruise the damsons well by pressing them against the side of the container with a large wooden spoon. Cover the wine with a thick cloth and leave for four days, stirring well once a day. Strain through your muslin, gently squeezing out all the liquid. Tip on the sugar and stir well till all has dissolved and add the yeast. Cover again and leave for a further four days. Strain off into the demijohn and fix the airlock. When it's time to bottle this off, top each bottle with a little brandy, using a wineglassful between all your bottles.

Cork well and try to leave for at least a year, when it will look and taste almost like port.

❧ *You can use quite a number of the wines in cooking – in things like* coq au vin, *in pâté and soups, steak and kidney pie, pork hot pot and many others.*

TWO DANDELION WINES

You will find dandelions blooming profusely from April through till June. The flowers must be freshly picked on a nice warm day.

[1]

This is one of the finest tonic wines, very good for those with a sluggish liver or indigestion. You will need quite a lot of dandelion *heads* for this, as it is wise to remove the little green collar round the flower head for this particular wine.

3 QUARTS DANDELION HEADS (*pressed down firmly in a jug*), 1 GALLON WATER, 3 lb SUGAR, 3 ORANGES, 1 OZ YEAST

Hold the dandelion head upside down, cut off the green part, and put the petals into your bucket. Pour a gallon of boiling water over them. Cover with a cloth and leave for two days. Then tip all this into a large saucepan, add the grated orange rind, bring to the boil and boil steadily for ten minutes. Cool a little and then strain into your bucket and add the sugar, stirring until it has dissolved. Add the juice from the oranges. When the wine has cooled add the yeast. Leave in the bucket, covered with a cloth, for four days. Then strain off into demi-john and fit the airlock. Bottle off when the wine has stopped working.

As well as being a 'tonic' wine this makes a very nice dinner wine. April 23rd, St George's day, is considered to be the best day for picking dandelions (provided it's not raining!).

This makes a lovely golden-coloured wine, suitable for drinking at any time – with or without meals. Dandelion wine usually turns out sweet or semi-sweet.

[2]

This recipe does not involve removing the little green frill from the back of the flower head. Nonetheless there must be *no* green stalks left on – otherwise the wine will have a very bitter taste.

3 QUARTS DANDELION HEADS, 4 lb SUGAR,
2 LEMONS, 1 ORANGE, 1 GALLON WATER, 1 OZ YEAST

Put the flower heads into your wine-making container and pour over them a gallon of boiling water. Cover closely and leave for three days, stirring each day. Then strain through your muslin. Pour into a large saucepan, and add the sugar and the grated rinds of the fruit. Bring up to the boil, simmer gently for about twenty minutes, then leave to cool a little. Put this all back into your bucket and add the juice of the fruit. When the wine is cool but not cold, sprinkle on the yeast. Cover again and leave for a further five days. Strain and pour into your demijohn and continue as on page 18.

This is drinkable at any time after six months – but try leaving it for a year.

TWO ELDERBERRY WINES

[1]

Late September and early October is the best time to pick elderberries.

> 3 lb ELDERBERRIES (*after removing the stalks*),
> 3 lb SUGAR, I GALLON WATER, I LEMON, $\frac{1}{2}$ OZ YEAST,
> I lb RAISINS (*for a sweeter wine*), I lb DAMSONS OR
> BLACKBERRIES (*optional*)

Pick your berries on a warm balmy autumn day – you can tell that they are truly ripe when the birds begin to eat them. To remove the berries from the stalks use the prongs of a table fork. Weigh them, put them into your bucket, pour on the gallon of boiling water and mash the berries against the side of the container with a large wooden spoon. Cover and leave for three or four days. Strain and tip the liquid back into your clean bucket, add the sugar and stir till you think it has all dissolved. Squeeze the lemon and add all the juice. Sprinkle on the yeast. Cover for three days, strain again and pour the wine into your demijohn, fix the airlock, and continue as on page 18.

This will produce a medium-dry wine, rich and full-bodied. Should you wish to make a sweeter wine, just add I lb raisins, split and chopped, when you add the boiling water at the beginning of the recipe.

You can also add I lb damsons or blackberries to this wine, at the same time as you add the elderberries. When this has matured it will taste almost like burgundy.

You can dry elderberries in the sun and then make a good non-alcoholic drink in wintertime by pouring water on them and adding sugar to taste. Excellent for a head cold.

[2]

This wine will have a rich spicy taste, and is excellent when mulled as a winter drink. Taken hot at bedtime it will induce sleep, and also help to sweat out a cold. And, of course, it makes a lovely rich red wine suitable for drinking with most meaty meals.

$3\frac{1}{2}$ lb ELDERBERRIES, 3 lb DEMERARA SUGAR,
1 lb RAISINS, $\frac{1}{2}$ OZ GROUND GINGER, 1 TEASPOON
CINNAMON, 4 CLOVES, $\frac{1}{2}$ OZ ROOT GINGER (*bruised*),
1 LEMON, 1 GALLON WATER, $\frac{1}{2}$ OZ YEAST

Strip the berries from the stalks, and weigh them. Put them into your bucket and pour the gallon of boiling water over them. Cover and let them stand for twenty-four hours. Bruise them well with a wooden spoon before straining them off. Measure the liquid, and to every gallon add the 3 lb sugar and thinly sliced lemon. Now boil up the cloves, raisins, cinnamon and the two lots of ginger in a little of the wine. Strain this and tip into the wine. Sprinkle on yeast. Cover with a thick cloth and leave for four days. Strain and pour the wine into the demijohn, fix the airlock, and continue as on page 18.

Drinkable within four months.

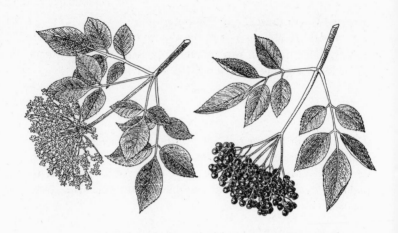

❧ *One old lady I knew always kept her red earthenware pan of wine under the kitchen table while it was working, because there was not much room in her tiny cottage. One day I went to see her just as she was taking a look at her fermenting dandelion wine. 'Ah,' she cried, 'I caught another little beggar, 'tis they mice you see, they gets in me wine pan after the toast [in the old days people always spread their yeast on a slice of toast] then they drowns in the wine. But I shan't take the mouse out,' she went on, 'that'll help work the wine.'*

In the old days it is said that Devon farmers used to throw a sheep's innards into their newly-made cider to help work it. Perhaps my friend came from that part of the country and was keeping up an old tradition!

TWO ELDERFLOWER WINES

[1]

This is best made in May and June, when the creamy flowers of the elder grow almost everywhere in the country.

2 PINTS ELDERFLOWER, 3 lb SUGAR, 2 LEMONS,
1 GALLON WATER, $\frac{1}{2}$ OZ YEAST

Be sure that it's a nice dry sunny day when you go out to gather your elderflowers. Put the elder florets into your wine-making bucket, with no bits of green on them at all. Add the grated rind of the lemons and the sugar, and pour over them a gallon of boiling water. Stir well and leave to cool. Add the lemon juice and the yeast, cover with a cloth and leave for three days. Strain, then tip into the demijohn, fix the airlock, and proceed as on page 18.

This will make a delicate light amber-coloured sweet wine, drinkable after six months.

[2]

This is best made in May or June.

2 PINTS ELDERFLOWER HEADS (*picked over so that no green at all remains*), 1 lb RAISINS (*the ones with pips in if possible. Split each one by opening them with your two thumbs*), THE JUICE OF A LARGE GRAPEFRUIT, 3 lb SUGAR, THE WHITE OF 1 EGG, 1 GALLON WATER, 1 OZ YEAST

Tip the sugar into a large saucepan, add the water and stir well. Beat up the white of egg and add, again stirring well. Boil for about twenty-five minutes. Take off from the heat and at once skim off any scum that has risen. Into your bucket put the elderflowers, picked over so that no green at all remains, the raisins and the grapefruit juice, and pour the warm liquid over them (the raisins should be those with pips in, if possible, and each one should be split open with the thumbs). When this has cooled down add the yeast. Cover the wine and leave in the bucket for the next four days, stirring it daily. Strain again into the demijohn and fix the airlock. Leave for at least a month before either bottling off or putting into a cask or stone jar.

A delicate, sweet pale amber-coloured wine, it should be ready to drink in six months.

❧ *A local farmer was given champagne at a party. When asked by his host how he liked his drink he replied, 'Ah 'tis a nice drop o' gooseberry wine, but it ent as good as my missus makes.'*

Gooseberry wine is known *as 'poor man's champagne'.*

GOOSEBERRY WINE

I like to use really ripe gooseberries to make my wine in May–
July, though some folk prefer them to be hard and green. You
will need

4 lb GOOSEBERRIES, 3 lb SUGAR, 1 GALLON WATER,
½ oz YEAST

Top and tail the gooseberries and put them into your bucket.
Pour over the boiling water and bruise the gooseberries well
with a large wooden spoon, or an old-fashioned wooden rolling
pin, pressing them against the side of the bucket. Cover with a
cloth and leave for a couple of days. Strain, squeezing out as
much of the juice as possible. Now add the sugar and the
yeast. Cover again and leave for five days. Strain again. Pour
the wine into the demijohn, fix the airlock and leave to ferment
in a warm room. Then bottle off.

Gooseberry wine is best left for at least a year. Sometimes it
will turn into a sparkling wine by accident. So watch it after
you have bottled it off, as sometimes a third fermentation will
take place. *If* this happens, re-bottle it off into champagne-
type bottles and lightly cork with plastic screw corks, which
can be eased if necessary. The wine should then be stored on
its side in a cool place.

GORSE WINE

'Kissing's out of fashion when the gorse is not in bloom': I don't know who first said it but whoever did so was right, because on the commons you can always find a few flowers out, even in the dead of winter. However, September is perhaps the best time to make gorse wine.

Gorse wine is reputed to be excellent for the kidneys, and in my grandmother's day it was often given to people with the 'dropsy'; but it also makes a nice dinner wine. Mine always seems to turn out a little on the dry side (I prefer sweet or semi-sweet wines), so if you like your wine dry try this one.

You will need gloves, a pair of scissors and an old clean white cotton pillowcase to drop the flowers into – if you do this carefully there will be no need to pick them over when you get home, and you can keep them in the pillowcase during the wine-making process. You will need

1 GALLON GORSE FLOWERS, 3 lb SUGAR,
2 LEMONS, 2 ORANGES, 1 GALLON WATER, ½ OZ YEAST

Keep the flowers in the bag or pillowcase, place them in a large saucepan, pour over half the boiling water and simmer for about fifteen minutes. Meanwhile boil up the rest of the water; tip this and the water from the saucepan into your wine-making container, after you have squeezed as much of the liquid as possible from the pillow case. Add the sugar and the grated rinds of both lemons and oranges; then add the juices from the lemons and oranges, stir well and leave to cool.

Add the yeast, cover and leave for a week. Then strain, and continue as directed on page 18.

This is well worth the 'prickles' that you might have to put up with when gathering the flowers. It is drinkable in six months and should be a rich golden colour.

GRAPEFRUIT WINE

This is one of the simplest wines to make, although of course it is a little expensive.

8 GRAPEFRUITS, 1 GALLON WATER, $3\frac{1}{2}$ lb SUGAR,
1 OZ YEAST

Slice the grapefruit – don't peel them, but remove the pips – and place in your bucket. Pour over them a gallon of cold water. Cover and leave for five days, stirring daily. Then strain and add the sugar and yeast. Cover again and leave for a couple of days. Pour into the demijohn and continue as directed on page 18.

This is a quick maturing wine, and will be ready to drink in four months. It is considered to be a good tonic and 'pick-me up' as well as a very pleasant dinner wine. This really tastes of grapefruit, and is a lovely golden colour.

GREENGAGE WINE

Late July and early August is the right time to make this – and just every so often we have a bumper crop of greengages. You will need

4 lb RIPE STONED GREENGAGES, I GALLON WATER,
3 lb SUGAR, ½ OZ YEAST, GIN

Halve the fruit, taking out the stones, and put the fleshy gages into your bucket. Pour over the boiling water. Cover and leave for five days. Strain off, adding the sugar, and stir well. Add the yeast to the liquid. Cover again and leave for at least a week. Pour into the demijohn, fix the airlock, let the wine ferment, and proceed as on page 18. Bottle off in the usual way, adding a tablespoon of gin to each bottle.

The wine should be ready to drink in six months. If you prefer a not-too-sweet wine cut down the amount of sugar to 2½ lb.

LAST OF THE SUMMER WINE

I made this one in August – it is a brand-new recipe which I created last summer.

1 lb EARLY BLACKBERRIES, 1 lb STONED EARLY
VICTORIA PLUMS, 1 lb SWEET-SCENTED ROSE PETALS,
3 lb SUGAR, 1 LEMON, 1 ORANGE, 1 GALLON WATER,
½ OZ YEAST

Take the stones from the plums and roll the blackberries in a cloth to clean them. Then place the rose petals, blackberries and plums into your wine-making bucket and pour over a gallon of boiling water. Cover with a thick cloth and leave for three days, stirring two or three times each day. Strain and squeeze out as much liquid as possible. Pour this liquid into your bucket and tip in the sugar, the juice and the rinds of both the lemon and orange, stir well until the sugar has dissolved, and then sprinkle on the yeast. Cover well and stand the bucket in a warm place. Leave for a week, then strain again and pour the wine into your demijohn. Proceed as on page 18.

This makes a delicate sweet wine with a slightly scented bouquet; it's a lovely pinky-red in colour. Drinkable after four months – just right for Christmas, in fact – its taste will bring a breath of summer into the dark days of winter.

MANGOLD WINE

It's a bit of a job to get hold of mangolds these days – not many farmers seem to grow them around here. But I know a good old-fashioned farmer who still grows a fair crop and I can rely on him to let me have a few for wine-making – providing that I present him with a bottle of the golden nectar when it's fit. I have to wait until the farmer opens his 'mango' bury in February or March before I can make this wine. You need

5 lb MANGOLDS, 2 ORANGES, 2 LEMONS, 3 lb SUGAR,
1 GALLON WATER, $\frac{1}{2}$ OZ YEAST

Wash the mangolds well but don't peel them. Cut them into small pieces, cover them with the water, bring to the boil, and simmer until tender. Strain the liquid and tip it back into the saucepan. Add the sugar and the rinds of the fruit and boil all this for about half an hour. Leave to cool. Add the juices from the fruit and sprinkle on the yeast. Cover and leave for three days. Strain, and then transfer the wine into the demijohn, fix the airlock and leave the wine to work, which will take about a month. Bottle off.

A lovely golden-coloured wine, a bit on the dry side, it can be drunk when it is six months old – but the longer you keep it the better it gets.

MARIGOLD WINE

August is a good month in which to make this wine. Marigolds take over my flower garden about this time, and from then till early October the garden is ablaze with them, smothering everything else in sight. The good thing is that I can gather a gallon of flower heads, and you can't see where I've picked them from! Try to pick your marigolds on a sunny day, preferable at midday. Then – it is said – that you will be actually bottling sunshine, and the bouquet of your wine will be much better for it.

1 GALLON MARIGOLD FLOWERS, 1 GALLON WATER,
3 lb SUGAR, $\frac{1}{2}$ OZ YEAST, 1 LEMON, $\frac{1}{2}$ lb HONEY,
$\frac{1}{2}$ pt WHITE WINE

Simmer the sugar, water and honey for about ten minutes, cool, and add the marigold flowers, cutting off as much of the green frill as possible. Add the juice and the rind of the lemon. Sprinkle the yeast on the top, cover and leave for five days. Strain and pour into the demijohn, and continue as on page 18. When the time comes to bottle this wine off, half a pint of any home-made white wine added to it will improve it no end.

The wine will be ready to drink in eight months.

MAY BLOSSOM WINE

May blossom, or hawthorn blossom, grows freely during the months of May and June.

1 QUART MAY BLOSSOM (*free of all stalks and any green*),
1 ORANGE, 3½ lb SUGAR, 1 GALLON WATER, ½ OZ YEAST

Pick the blossoms when they are full out but not falling. Boil up the water, sugar and grated orange peel for about fifteen minutes. Leave to cool a little and then add the may blossoms and the juice of the orange. When quite cool add the yeast. Cover the wine and leave for four days, stirring twice daily. Strain and continue as directed on page 18.

This makes a delicate pale creamy wine that is drinkable in six months.

MEADOWSWEET WINE

Meadowsweet blooms freely all summer long, so you can pick your time as when to make it.

'Meadowsweet makes the heart merry' someone once wrote, and indeed this wine certainly does that. The foamy cream flowers have a sweet drowsy smell, which seems to embody the essence of the countryside in summer. You will need

1 GALLON MEADOWSWEET FLOWERS, 3 lb SUGAR,
½ lb RAISINS, 2 LEMONS, 2 TABLESPOONS COLD
STRONG TEA, 1 GALLON WATER, ½ OZ YEAST

You need to pick these flowers before they are overblown. Be sure that no green is left on the florets. Place them in your wine-making bucket along with the sugar, raisins (split) and the grated lemon rind. Pour over the boiling water, and stir well until the sugar has dissolved. Leave to get a little cool and then add the lemon juice and the cold tea. When really cool sprinkle on the yeast. Cover well and leave for ten days. Strain and pour into your demijohn, proceed as on page 18.

A creamy-amber wine, this will be drinkable in six months.

MIXED FRUIT WINE

This wine can be made in June or July. When the soft fruit have passed their best and I think I've made enough jam and jelly, then I use the 'tail end' fruit to make a super mixed fruit wine, which includes gooseberries, raspberries, black and red-currant, and, if there are any left, a few strawberries.

4 lb MIXED FRUIT (*they don't have to be in equal quantities*),
1 GALLON BOILING WATER, 4 lb SUGAR, 2 LEMONS,
½ OZ YEAST

Top and tail the fruit and place in your wine-making container. Add the boiling water, cover and leave for three days, stirring three times a day. Strain, put back into your container, and add the sugar, the juice and the grated rinds of the lemons. Stir well till the sugar has dissolved, and then sprinkle on the yeast. Cover again, and leave for a week. Strain and tip the wine into the demijohn, and continue as on page 18.

This makes a delicious rich fruity wine, sweet, and a lovely colour; it should be ready to drink in six months.

A TALE OF WOE

❧ *My Auntie Sarah was a great wine-maker. She was also a good chapel-going body too. One hot summer I remember she had a couple of lay preachers staying with her for a few days. They were going round to some of the remote villages to preach the gospel and made my auntie's home their temporary headquarters. Both were very much the 'holier than thou' type and firmly believed that any form of 'drink' was a sure passport to hell.*

Before they arrived at the farm we carefully moved all the bottles and casks of wine up into a loft over the kitchen. The farm had once been a mill and this loft was where they had stored the flour. We had to handle it very gently because some of the wine was still at the fermenting stage, but at least it was out of sight.

All we heard from the lay preachers was the hell fire and damnation that would surely be the fate of anyone who took any sort of intoxicating drink. My uncle would catch my eye and look heavenwards as if to say, 'How much longer have we got to put up with this?'

But suddenly their visit was cut short. The afternoon was very hot, distant thunder rolled round the hills. There was not a breath of air anywhere, and the worthy gentlemen were leading off for the umpteenth time about the sins of the world, and how they were going to convert everybody, when the air was shattered with a loud report, then another and another. Up jumped the black-coated lay preachers, eyes blazing, arms flung heavenwards. 'There are the warning notes,' called one. 'Yes, hell fire and damnation!' shouted the other: 'Judgement on all sinners!'

Just at that moment a red, gory substance started pouring down

the walls and onto the white, scrubbed stone floor and settled in a puddle at one of the visitors' feet, and a strong fruity, winey smell filled the room. I took one look at my red-faced aunt and we both went off to get buckets and house flannels to sop up the mess. The visitors stamped out of the house and up the road toward the next village and we never saw them again.

The only damnation came from my uncle because his favourite wine (raspberry, red and blackcurrant) had ended up all over the kitchen floor.

MONKSWOOD MEAD

The best time to make mead is during the summer months –
say May, June or July. The old name for mead is metheglin
and I've often heard my Grannie say, 'Try a drop o' me
metheglin, 'tis supposed to be the nectar of heaven.' Mead was
also made by monks, and I have called this one Monkswood
mead after the field where the great Eynsham Abbey once
stood.

I GALLON WATER, 3 lb RUNNY HONEY, ½ OZ YEAST,
2 CLOVES, I TEASPOON CINNAMON, I SMALL BUNCH
HERBS (*Parsley, thyme and marjoram*)

Place the water, honey, herbs and spices in a large saucepan
and bring to the boil. Simmer for half an hour, top up with
water to keep the volume up to the gallon. Skim any scum
that forms. When the liquid is cool, sprinkle on the yeast and
leave in your bucket or pan for three days, covered closely.
Then strain and pour into your demijohn and proceed as on
page 18.

The mead will be drinkable after two months.

NETTLE WINE

This wine is best made any time from April till the end of May, because that's when the nettles are young and green. It is not to be confused with 'nettle beer', which is quite a different thing and can be found in the 'summer drinks' section.

1 QUART NETTLE TOPS, 2 LEMONS, 4 lb SUGAR,
½ OZ ROOT GINGER, 1 GALLON WATER, ½ OZ YEAST

Rinse the nettle tops under the tap, place them in a large saucepan, and cover with water. Add the rind of the lemons and the bruised ginger. Bring to the boil and simmer for thirty minutes: if you think that you have lost much liquid in boiling, make up to the gallon with cold water. Put the sugar into your wine-making bucket, pour over the hot liquid and add the juices of the lemons. Stir and leave to cool before adding the yeast. Cover and leave for three days before straining the wine off into your demijohn. Continue as directed on page 18.

This will be a pale greeny amber wine, drinkable in six months. Apart from being very pleasant to drink, it is also good for clearing the blood and easing the digestion.

OAK LEAF WINE

The leaves of the oak tree should be picked when they are young and at their best – about the third week in June is quite a good time.

1 GALLON OAK LEAVES (*measured in a jug*), 3½ lb SUGAR,
2 SWEET ORANGES, 2 LEMONS, 1 GALLON WATER,
½ OZ YEAST

Boil up the sugar with water and pour it over the oak leaves. Cover and leave overnight. Then add the juices from the oranges and lemons, and the yeast. Cover again for two days, then strain and tip the wine into your demijohn. Carry on as directed on page 18.

A medium dry white wine with a good bouquet, drinkable after six months.

ORANGE WINE

This is quite an expensive wine which acts as a tonic and is recommended to people suffering from anaemia: people who work in the orange groves and eat plenty of the fruit, seldom suffer from influenza or anaemia.

12 ORANGES, 1 GALLON WATER, 2 lb SUGAR,
½ OZ YEAST

Cut the oranges in thin slices, remove the pips, and put them into your wine-making container. Cover with boiling water. Cover and leave for five days, stirring daily. Strain and add the sugar, stir well, and add just a sprinkling of yeast about half an ounce). Leave for a further three days. Tip all into your demijohn and continue as on page 18.

This wine will be drinkable in three months, but of course it will mature and improve if left longer.

PARSLEY BRANDY WINE

Parsley makes a delightful amber-coloured sweet wine, which would improve any meal; and the fact that the leaves contain vitamin C means that it is bound to 'do a body a power of good'. So here's a recipe which is very simple and gives a wonderful result.

½ lb PARSLEY LEAVES (*free from stalks*), ¼ lb RAISINS
PULLED OPEN (*these give the wine a 'brandy' colour*),
2 ORANGES, 2 LEMONS, 3½ lb SUGAR, 1 OZ ROOT
GINGER (*bruised*), 1 GALLON WATER, ½ OZ YEAST

Wash the parsley and tip it into a large saucepan. Cover with the water, bring to the boil and simmer for half an hour, keeping the water topped up to one gallon. Strain and tip into your wine-making container and add the bruised ginger, raisins, sugar, rinds and juice of the lemons and oranges. Stir until the sugar has dissolved. When cool add the yeast. Cover with a cloth and leave for a week. Then strain again into the demijohn and proceed as on page 18. Bottle off.

This wine will be drinkable in four months and is truly outstanding amongst home-made wines. It has a most delicate bouquet and makes a delicious dinner or lunch-time wine.

PARSLEY WINE

This wine can be made at almost any time of the year – whenever you have sufficient parsley growing in your garden.

1 lb PARSLEY (*free from stalks*), 2 ORANGES, 2 LEMONS, 4 lb SUGAR, A PIECE OF ROOT GINGER AS BIG AS A WALNUT, 1 GALLON WATER, ½ OZ YEAST

Put your parsley into your wine bucket and pour a gallon of boiling water over it. Cover and let it stand for two days. Strain and boil up the liquor for twenty minutes along with the ginger and the grated rinds of the fruit. Pour the hot liquor onto the sugar, add the juice and when cool add the yeast. Leave for four days. Strain, pour into the demijohn, and proceed as on page 18.

This wine should be ready in six months – but of course it will improve if you can manage to keep it longer, as all wines improve if kept for a year or more.

A farm worker was given a bottle of home-made wine by his rather mean employer. When he was asked what he thought of it he said, 'If 'twas any worse I couldn't have drunk it, and if it had been any better I shouldn't have had the chance!'

PARSNIP WINE

The first wine I make, at the beginning of the year, is parsnip. This is when they are at their best, when the frosts have turned some of the starch into sugar. However, one old lady I know only ever uses young parsnips.

For anyone who has lost his appetite, a glass of parsnip wine a day will soon lead to an improvement in his eating habits. Some people call parsnip wine 'mock sherry', for it looks and often tastes like it.

4 lb PARSNIPS, 1 GALLON WATER, 4 lb DEMERARA
SUGAR (3 *lb for a dry wine*), 2 LEMONS,
2 GRAPEFRUITS, $\frac{1}{2}$ OZ YEAST

Scrub the parsnips clean but do not peel. Cut up into chunks and place in a large saucepan along with the cold water and the thinly sliced but unpeeled lemons and grapefruit. Cook until the parsnips are tender but not mushy. Strain the liquor onto the sugar and stir well. When cool, sprinkle on the yeast. Cover with a thick cloth and leave for ten days. Strain, tip into demijohn and proceed as on page 18.

Try not to drink this until it has stood for a year. If you make it in January it should be just fit to drink at Christmas time.

PEAR WINE OR PERRY

You can make this wine during August and September.

Whether you call this pear wine or perry, the end product is much the same. Although pears are not credited with any great medicinal value, it is said that sufferers of gout or those with gout tendencies should drink pear wine. The recipe is simple –

4 lb RIPE PEARS, 3 lb SUGAR, 1 GALLON WATER,
¼ OZ YEAST

For this wine you need only a sprinkling of yeast, for the ripe pears will soon help to set up fermentation.

Remove the stalks from the fruit. Put the pears into your wine-making vessel and pour cold water over them. Cover and leave for a week, stirring a couple of times a day, pressing the fruit against the side of your bucket with a wooden spoon. Strain off, add the sugar to the juice, sprinkle on the yeast and leave in your bucket for a further four days, with the wine *well* covered. Tip all into your demijohn and proceed as directed on page 18.

Last year I made two separate gallons of pear wine, one one day and the other two days afterwards. I used exactly the same method, but the first gallon cleared within two weeks of being in the demijohn, while the second batch remained quite cloudy. I mentioned this to an eighty-nine-year-old wine-making neighbour, and he suggested adding to my cloudy gallon a spoonful of *his* 'pectolytic enzyme' which he had bought from the chemist, which I did. Whether that did the job or, given time, the wine had cleared itself, I shall never know, but it turned out lovely and clear and is a very nice wine.

Perry should be drinkable in five months, but will improve if it is kept a year or more.

❧ *One elderly man that I knew used to 'test' his new wine by drinking a mug of it (I wouldn't recommend this, because the new wine would still be working and so bound to upset the stomach). He took me into his old dairy one day where there were three big red earthenware pans, covered with old blankets. He lifted the cover from the first pan, and with his great gnarled hand he scooped the 'head' off the working wine and dipped an old enamelled mug into it. Then he drank the mug full down in one gulp. 'Ah needs a few more days yet, he remarked, before proceeding to drink a mug full from the other two pans without batting an eyelid.*

'Won't it upset your stomach?' I asked.

'God bless 'e no,' he replied. 'That keeps I as fit as a fighting cock.'

PEA POD WINE

Summer is the time for making this one.

This is an easy wine to make, and it's a pity to throw those lovely fresh green pea pods onto the compost heap when they could be made into a delightful wine that is supposed to resemble hock.

5 lb PEA PODS, 3 lb SUGAR, JUICE OF A LARGE
GRAPEFRUIT, I GALLON WATER, $\frac{1}{2}$ OZ YEAST

Wash the pods and boil them up in the gallon of water until they are quite tender. Strain and add the sugar to the liquid. When nearly cool add the juice of the grapefruit and the yeast. Next day tip the wine into your demijohn and continue as on page 18.

Drinkable within four months.

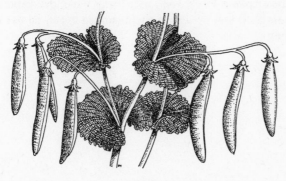

PLUM WINE

August and early September are the best times for making plum wine. Plums halved and stoned freeze well, so if you haven't time to make the wine while the plums are fresh, freeze some and make it later in the year.

3 lb STONED VICTORIA PLUMS, 3 lb SUGAR,
1 GALLON WATER, ½ OZ YEAST

Put the plums into your bucket and pour a gallon of boiling water over them. Cover and leave for five days stirring a couple of times daily. Strain, and pour the liquid back into the bucket. Stir in the sugar and keep stirring until the sugar has dissolved, then sprinkle on the yeast and cover the wine with a thick cloth. Stand the wine in a warm place – in the kitchen window might do. Strain again and tip all the wine into your demijohn. Proceed as on page 18.

Plums make a lovely rich, red, fruity wine, drinkable after six months. If you prefer your wine not so sweet, on use 2¼ lb of sugar.

POTATO WINES

There are several ways of making potato wine, all of which involve mixing in other ingredients such as prunes, raisins, figs, and wheat. I think potato and raisin is my favourite – the end product could easily be taken for a hock.

6 OLD RAW POTATOES THE SIZE OF EGGS, 2 ORANGES,
3 LEMONS, 4 lb SUGAR, $\frac{1}{2}$ lb RAISINS, 1 GALLON WATER
$\frac{1}{2}$ OZ DRIED YEAST, OR A PIECE OF YEAST AS BIG AS
A WALNUT

Thinly slice the oranges and lemons and remove the pips, cut up the potatoes into chunks, and pull open the raisins. Put into your bucket with the sugar, and pour over the gallon of water. Stir well. Sprinkle the yeast on top, cover and leave for ten days. Strain and tip into your demijohn and proceed as on page 18.

This whisky-coloured wine is best left a year before drinking.

QUINCE WINE

Autumn is the time to make this wine.

This is a simple wine to make, and a very pleasant one. Sufferers from rheumatism and gout can drink it freely knowing that it will not irritate their complaint.

2 DOZEN QUINCE, 1 GALLON WATER, 2 LEMONS,
3 lb SUGAR, $\frac{1}{2}$ OZ YEAST

Peel the quinces and chop them up quite small. Cover with water, bring to the boil and simmer for about twenty minutes. When cool, strain and tip the liquor into your bucket, adding the sugar, the juice of the lemons and the yeast. Cover and leave for three or four days. Tip all into your demijohn and continue as on page 18.

Quince is a slow maturing wine, and is better if left for at least a year before drinking.

RASPBERRY WINE

June and July are the best months to make this wine from fresh fruit. But raspberries freeze well, and wine made from frozen fruit turns out as good as that made from fresh raspberries.

3 lb RASPBERRIES, 3 lb SUGAR, 1 GALLON WATER,
½ oz YEAST

Choose firm ripe raspberries. Place them in a bucket and pour over them a gallon of boiling water. Cover with a cloth and leave for four days, stirring daily. Strain and tip the wine back into your wine-making bucket, add the sugar and stir well. Sprinkle on the yeast and cover again and stand the wine in a warm place. Leave for a week and then strain again and pour the wine into your demijohn. Proceed as on page 18.

Raspberries make one of the most aromatic fruit wines. It is also very refreshing, a rose-type wine that is delicious served with your sweet on a summer evening after you have kept it for a year: but it is drinkable after six months.

RHUBARB WINE

Don't use very young rhubarb for this wine, nor leave it till
the stalks are hard and tough: late May or early June should
be about the right time. An old lady once told me, 'Don't
make yer rhubarb wine till the leaves be as big as an elephant's
ear'. In other words never use young rhubarb for wine-
making, but wait until its more mature. You will need

4 lb RHUBARB, 3½ lb SUGAR, 1 GALLON WATER,
½ OZ YEAST, AND A PIECE OF ROOT GINGER AS BIG AS A
WALNUT

Wipe the rhubarb with a cloth and cut it into small pieces –
don't peel it. Pour over a gallon of boiling water, add the
ginger, cover and leave for four days, stirring each day. Strain,
add the sugar, stir until dissolved, then sprinkle on the yeast,
cover and leave for a further two days. Then strain off into
your demijohn and proceed as on page 18. This is a semi-
sweet wine, lovely served with ice on hot summer evenings.
Drinkable after six months.

ROSE HIP WINE

September or October are the best times to make this wine. For this wine I use the hips of the wild dog-rose, but I suppose rose-hips from the garden would do just as well. Rose hips are full of vitamin C and make a delicious deep rosé wine.

3 lb ROSE HIPS (*gathered after the first frost of autumn*),
1 ORANGE, 3 lb SUGAR, 1 GALLON WATER, ½ OZ YEAST

Wipe the fruit over by rolling them in a dry tea towel. Chop them roughly in half, and add the sugar. Pour boiling water over them. Cover and leave for a couple of days, stirring twice daily and crushing them against the side of the bucket with a wooden spoon. Now add the juice from the orange and sprinkle on the yeast. Cover and leave in a warm room for a further week. Strain, pour the liquid into the demijohn, and proceed as on page 18. Two ounces of dried figs first soaked in water to plim them up and added at the beginning will give a little more 'body' to the wine. Drinkable within three months.

TWO ROSE PETAL WINES

[1]

This can be made all through the summer. There is no need to pick the roses when they are at their best, but when they are just about to fall – so you are only saving them from the compost heap.

This is a most delightful and delicate wine, unlike any other; it will bring a breath of summer to a wintertime meal. Red rose petals are the best, and the heavier scented the better – though a mixture of red, pink and yellow will make a nicely coloured wine.

2 QUARTS ROSE PETALS, 3 lb SUGAR, 1 LEMON,
1 ORANGE, 1 GALLON WATER, ½ OZ YEAST,
A HANDFUL OF RAISINS

Place the rose petals in your wine-making vessel and pour over the boiling water. Stir well and leave for two days, covered. Strain and add the chopped raisins, the juice of the lemon and orange, and the sugar, and stir well. Sprinkle on the yeast, cover and leave for two days. Then strain again, pour into your demijohn, and proceed as on page 18.

The wine will be drinkable within six months, but even better by the time the roses bloom the following year. Lovely served at a summer luncheon party.

2 QUARTS ROSE PETALS (*the stronger scented and brighter coloured the better*), 2½ lb SUGAR, I LEMON, I GALLON WATER, ½ OZ YEAST

Bring the water to the boil. Add the sugar, rose petals, and juice of the lemon, and stir well. When it has cooled, add the yeast. Leave to ferment for a week, stirring daily and keeping closely covered. Then strain into a demijohn and proceed as on page 18.

Both rose petals wines have a delicate bouquet, are slightly scented, and are pale pinky amber in colour. Drinkable after six months.

RUNNER BEAN WINE

You can make this wine from July until September.

4 lb RUNNER BEANS, 2 LEMONS, 4 OZ RAISINS, 3 lb
SUGAR, 1 GALLON WATER, 2 TABLESPOONS STRONG
TEA LEAVES, ½ OZ YEAST

Cut the beans in half and place in a saucepan. Add the lemon rinds and water, bring to the boil and simmer for a quarter of an hour. Strain and pour the liquid over the sugar, the juice of the lemons, the roughly chopped raisins and the tea leaves. Leave to cool, and then sprinkle on the yeast. Cover well and leave for three days. Strain again, tip into demijohn and proceed as on page 18.

This wine is drinkable after four months.

❧ OLD WIVES' TALE: *If your wine will not clear add a table-spoon of whipped white of an egg to it.*

SAGE WINE

One of the most valuable wines for those suffering from anaemia, and a delicious dinner wine into the bargain.

1 lb SAGE LEAVES, 1 lb RAISINS, 3 lb DEMERARA
SUGAR, 1 GALLON WATER, $\frac{1}{2}$ OZ YEAST

Remove any stalks from the sage and put it into your wine-making bucket. Add the chopped raisins and the sugar. Cover with the gallon of water, which has been boiled and cooled. Stir till the sugar has dissolved and then add the yeast. Cover and leave for four days, stirring twice a day. Then strain, pour into the demijohn, and continue as on page 18.

A glass of this wine will aid the digestion, and help to clear the blood. (A bread-and-butter sandwich filled with sage will greatly help a person suffering from flatulence.) Drinkable after six months.

SLOE WINE

This wine is best made in October when there has been a frost or two – the sloes show up on the bushes because by then most of the leaves have fallen off.

The recipe was given to me many years ago by an elderly lady who lived in the village. Her cottage was so small that she had to keep her wine on the stairs, and they were those twisty stairs at that. On every step there were bottles of wine. 'We 'as to be a bit careful when we goes to bed' she told me, 'specially when we've been drinking some o' my ten-year-old.'

3 lb SLOES, I GALLON BOILING WATER,
4 lb SUGAR (*if you want it dry, add less*), ½ oz YEAST,
2 WINE GLASSES OF BRANDY

Pick off any stalks and wipe the sloes in a clean tea towel. Place them in your wine-making vessel and pour the boiling water over them. Cover and leave for five days, stirring daily, lightly crushing the sloes against the side of the container with a wooden spoon. Then strain, add the sugar and stir. Add the yeast, cover again and leave for a week. Tip all into your demijohn and continue as on page 18. When bottling off, divide two wine glasses of brandy between the bottles.

Try and leave it for a year, if you can. This makes a strong, full-bodied wine, rich and red, lovely served with pheasant or good English beef.

STRAWBERRY WINE

Make this whenever strawberries are available.

If you are like me and pick more than you really need at those 'pick your own' farms, it's a good idea to use the very best fruit for jam-making or eating and the rest to make delicious wine.

4 lb STRAWBERRIES, I GALLON WATER, 3 lb SUGAR, JUICE OF 2 LEMONS, $\frac{1}{2}$ OZ YEAST, A WINE GLASS OF WHISKY

Place the fruit in the wine-making vessel and mash against the side with a wooden spoon. Then pour over the cold water and leave covered for two days. Strain and add the lemon juice and the sugar. Stir well before adding the yeast. Cover and leave for four days before straining off into your demijohn. Proceed as on page 18. When you bottle this wine off, a wine glass of whisky divided between the bottles will help to produce a super wine.

The wine should be ready to drink in six months.

TWO TEA WINES

[1]

4 TABLESPOONS DRY TEALEAVES, JUICE AND RIND OF
1 LEMON, 2½ lb SUGAR, 1 GALLON WATER, ½ OZ YEAST

Some of the scented Indian and China teas make lovely clear,
dry wines. Pour the boiling water over the tea and sugar, stir
well, and leave until cool. Add the juice and rind of a lemon
and the yeast, cover and leave for two days. Strain and pour
into demijohn. Fit an air-lock, and proceed as on page 18.

Because this wine does not have the bouquet of other wines
it is a good one for blending with, say, a very dry wine, but
don't do this until you are ready to drink it – which should be
six months after you have made it.

[2]

Another very simple wine to make. You will need

1 GALLON TEA (*any type will do*), 1 lb RAISINS,
4 lb SUGAR, JUICE OF 4 LEMONS, JUICE OF 2 GRAPE-
FRUITS, 1 OZ YEAST

Save any tea left over from the teapot until you have collected
one gallon. Strain off any leaves. Add the sugar and the lemon

and grapefruit juice to the liquid. Stir well till all the sugar has dissolved. Chop up the raisins and add them also, along with the yeast. Cover and leave in the warm for five days. Strain off, pour into the demijohn, and proceed as on page 18. Drinkable after six months.

WALNUT LEAF WINE

You can make this wine in early spring, when the leaves are young and green, or in late July, when they are beginning to turn yellow.

> 1 GALLON WALNUT LEAVES (*loosely packed in a measuring jug*), 3 lb SUGAR, JUICE OF 2 LEMONS, $\frac{1}{2}$ lb HONEY, 1 GALLON WATER, $\frac{1}{2}$ OZ YEAST

Bring the water to the boil and dissolve the sugar and honey in it. When this clears, pour it boiling over the leaves. Infuse overnight. The next day strain, and add the lemon juice and yeast. Cover and leave for two or three days. Strain, tip into your demijohn and continue as on page 18.

This will make a delicate light wine with a subtle flavour; it should be drinkable in three months.

WHEAT AND RAISIN WINE

You can make this wine any time after the grain harvest is in.
I often wait until January or February to make mine.

   1 lb WHEAT (*cadged from a farmer*), 1 lb CHOPPED
   RAISINS, 1 lb CHOPPED AND PEELED OLD POTATOES,
   4 lb SUGAR, 1 GALLON WATER, 1 OZ YEAST

Put the wheat, chopped raisins, potatoes and sugar into your
wine-making bucket and cover with a gallon of cold *boiled*
water. Sprinkle on the yeast, cover with a cloth and leave for
two weeks. Stir gently once a day with a wooden spoon.
Strain, pour into demijohn, and proceed as on page 18.

   This makes a wonderful wine which tastes and looks almost
like whisky, and can be drunk after six months.

❧ *Let us have wine women mirth and laughter*
   Sermons and soda water the day after
                                    LORD BYRON 1788–1824

COOL DRINKS
for
WARM NIGHTS
and
HOT DAYS

APPLE DRINK

Take five or six good big cooking apples and slice them thinly.
Don't peel them or remove the cores. Put the sliced apples in
a saucepan, together with the rind and juice of one lemon and
two large cups of water. Cook till soft and then add half a
pound of sugar. Leave to get cold, then strain. A refreshing
drink, and very good for sufferers from constipation. Dilute if
necessary.

❧ OLD WIVES' TALE: *Use the peel from a sour apple to remove
warts. Gently rub the wart daily, and it will soon disappear.*

APPLE DASH

I BOTTLE HOME-MADE APPLE WINE (*see page* 28),
I lb SLICED PEACHES (*tinned peaches will do*),
2 SMALL GLASSES OF BRANDY, I BOTTLE FIZZY
LEMONADE, SUGAR, ICE

Put the sliced peaches in a bowl and cover with the apple wine
and brandy. Leave for two hours. Just before serving add sugar
to taste, then the lemonade and ice.

CHERRY CHEER

I BOTTLE SWEET RED HOME-MADE WINE (*sloe or blackcurrant, see pages* 82 *and* 34), I BOTTLE PARSLEY BRANDY WINE (*see page* 66), 4 TABLESPOONS CHERRY BRANDY, I lb STONED CHERRIES, SUGAR TO TASTE, GINGER ALE, ICE

Pour all the liquids over the cherries. Add sugar to taste. Chill for an hour in fridge and serve with ice and ginger ale.

CUCUMBER COBBLER

1 MEDIUM SIZE CUCUMBER, 4 TABLESPOONS CASTER
SUGAR, 1 LEMON, 3 TABLESPOONS BRANDY, $\frac{1}{2}$ PINT
WHITE WINE (*elderflower is nice – see page* 47), 1 BOTTLE
RED WINE (*blackberry would do – see page* 33), SODA
WATER, ICE

Thinly slice the cucumber and place in a bowl, along with the
juice of the lemon and the peel (very thin). Cover with the
sugar and mash all together with a wooden spoon. Add the
brandy and the red and white wines. Cover the bowl with a
tea towel, and put it in the fridge for an hour. Before serving
add the ice and soda water. Remove the lemon peel at the last
moment.

DANDELION SUMMER DRINK

3 QUARTS DANDELION PETALS, 2 lb SUGAR,
1 GALLON WATER, 2 LEMONS

Put the dandelion petals, lemon rinds and water into a large saucepan. Simmer together for half an hour, topping up with water to make up for any boiling away. Strain and add the sugar and lemon juice and stir well. Bottle off. This will not keep for very long, but it is best kept in the fridge once you have started on a bottle. Lovely served with ice cubes on a very hot day.

ELDERBERRY WATER

A delightful and refreshing drink for children. You require

1 lb RIPE ELDERBERRIES, SUGAR TO TASTE,
JUICE OF A LEMON, BOILING WATER

Strip the stalks from the elderberries. Put the elderberries in a quart jug, and add about eight ounces of caster sugar and the juice of a lemon. Top up with boiling water. Stir and leave to get cold. Strain through muslin and squeeze out all the liquid. This will keep quite well for five or six days.

ELDERFLOWER CHAMPAGNE

3 HEADS OF ELDERFLOWERS (*no green*), 1½ lb CASTER
SUGAR, 2 TABLESPOONS WHITE WINE VINEGAR,
1 LEMON, 1 GALLON WATER

Put the blossoms into a bowl or bucket. Sprinkle over the
lemon juice and the grated rind, along with the sugar and wine
vinegar. Add a gallon of cold water. Cover and leave for
twenty-four hours. Strain into bottles and leave for two weeks
before drinking, when it should be clear and sparkling. This is
a delightful refreshing summer drink but will only keep for a
matter of a few weeks – through the hot summer weather.
Store the bottles on their side in a cool place.

ELDERFLOWER CHAMPAGNE CORDIAL

25 ELDERFLOWER HEADS (*no green*), 4 ORANGES,
3 lb SUGAR, 4 PINTS WATER, I LEMON, 2 OZ TARTARIC
ACID

Boil the water and leave till cool. Then pour this over the
heads of the elderflowers picked free from green, sugar,
tartaric acid and the finely sliced oranges and lemon. Leave
for forty-eight hours then strain and bottle off. Use diluted. A
delightful summer drink.

HARVESTERS' DRINK

I LEMON, I GRAPEFRUIT, I ORANGE, I GALLON
WATER, $\frac{1}{4}$ lb FINE OATMEAL

Grate the rinds from the fruit and put them into a saucepan. Add the juice from the fruit, along with the oatmeal and sugar and two pints of water. Bring to the boil and simmer for ten minutes. Take off the heat and add the rest of the water. Stir well, strain when cold. A refreshing harvest-time drink.

❧ *In the days when the corn was all cut with scythes there would be six or seven men at a time scything away in a field at harvest time, and in those days 'twas right and proper for the farmer who employed them to supply a certain amount of beer or cider for the men. And every now and then the gang of thirsty workers would stop and take a swig from the big stone jar, the sort with a handle near the narrow neck. The jar was always kept either in a cool ditch or in the shade of a tree.*

And one of the scything gang used to tell the tale about how they cured one of the chaps who was a bit on the greedy side. Jimmy his name was, and they reckoned that he had twice as much drink from that jar than the others did. So they played a trick on him. One day they came across a nest of new born mice, so they dropped them into the beer jar, which they knew was nearly empty, and waited for Jimmy to make a bee-line for the jar. He took a good long swig and finished the lot and wiped his mouth with the back of his hand, then he said, 'That beer's got a bit thick, I reckon farmer's got to the bottom of the barrel, that last drop had hops in I know.'

MIDSUMMER MAGIC

I BOTTLE OF SWEET RED WINE (*cherry or blackberry*),
I BOTTLE OF WHITE MEDIUM SWEET WINE (*elderflower
or dandelion*), I lb STRAWBERRIES, I lb RASPBERRIES,
I ORANGE (*thinly sliced*), 2 SWEET APPLES (*thinly sliced*),
SUGAR TO TASTE, 2 TABLESPOONS CHERRY
BRANDY, ICE CUBES

Put all the fruit in a large bowl and cover with all the liquids.
Stir in sugar to taste and chill. Serve with ice cubes.

NETTLE BEER

This is a very wholesome drink which clears the blood and strengthens the digestion, and one that country folk relied on years before the health service. It is equally good to drink today. In spring when the green nettles are young and at their best, then's the time to make your nettle beer – and you will need

2 lb NETTLE TOPS (*just the green tops of the nettle*),
2 LEMONS, I GALLON WATER, I lb DEMERARA SUGAR,
I OZ CREAM OF TARTAR, $\frac{1}{2}$ OZ YEAST

Rinse the nettles under the tap. Put them into a saucepan with the water. Bring to the boil and simmer for fifteen minutes. Then strain. Put the rind and the juice of the lemon, and the sugar and the cream of tartar into a bowl. Stir well and add them to the liquid. Add the yeast when the liquid is cool but not cold. Cover and keep in a warm room for a couple of days. Strain into strong bottles, and don't cork too tightly; strong bottles are a 'must' – cider bottles will do – as the drink becomes gassy. Keep at least a week before drinking.

NETTLE SYRUP

This again is a good blood purifier, and makes a very pleasant summer drink, especially when soda water is added to it.

2 lb YOUNG NETTLE TOPS, 4 PINTS WATER, SUGAR

Pick the young nettle tops on a fine day, and rinse them under the tap. Put into a saucepan, along with the water. Bring to the boil and simmer for about an hour, replacing water that has boiled away. Strain when fairly cool and add one pound of sugar to every pint of liquid. Stir well. Bottle off when cold.

SUMMER SPECIAL

A lunchtime treat.

1 BOTTLE SWEET RED WINE – (*blackcurrant is
recommended – see page* 34), 4 TABLESPOONS BRANDY,
1 lb RIPE STRAWBERRIES, 2 BOTTLES FIZZY
LEMONADE

Soak the strawberries in the brandy overnight, then add the
wine and cool in fridge. Just before serving add the lemonade.
Super!

❧ *Faggot Thomas reckoned that he drank a pint of his wife's home-
made wine before breakfast every morning of his life. But if he had
another pint in the evening then he began to feel light-headed.*

*Anyhow, one night he and his old pal Thatcher Adams had been
celebrating the fact that Thatcher's wife had just had her tenth child,
and when it came to going home Faggot had difficulty in putting one
foot before the other. He was crawling up the street on all fours when
he met Sid Smith. 'Oh dear,' Sid said, you are in a state, 'can I give
you a hand?' 'T'nt a hand I wants, you silly old begger, 'tis a pair of
new legs, these old 'uns of mine refuses to work.'*

HOT PUNCHES
for
COLD NIGHTS

Your guests will appreciate a drink of hot punch or mulled wine just before they go home on a cold frosty night. Here are a few ideas that are not too lethal, using your home-made wines. Serve in strong heat-proof cups or glasses.

BLACKBERRY AND
CRAB APPLE PUNCH

1 PINT BLACKBERRY WINE (*see page* 33), 1 PINT CRAB APPLE WINE (*see page* 40). Or any good red wine – cherry, sloe or elderberry, 1 LEMON, THINLY SLICED, 1 ORANGE, THINLY SLICED, 6 CLOVES, 1 TEASPOON GROUND GINGER, 1 TEASPOON MIXED SPICE, 1 TEASPOON GRATED NUTMEG, 12 OZ DEMERARA SUGAR

Put all the ingredients into a large saucepan and *almost* bring to the boil, stirring all the while. Strain into a punch bowl or similar container. Serve at once.

CHRISTMAS CRACKER

2 PINTS OF WINE — (*elderberry and sloe recommended see pages 44 and 82*), 1 ROASTED LEMON STUCK WITH A DOZEN CLOVES, 8 OZ DEMERARA SUGAR, 1 HEAPED TEASPOON CINNAMON, 2 ORANGES, THINLY SLICED, 1 EXTRA ORANGE

Roast the lemon stuck with cloves in a hot oven for about half an hour. Bring from the oven hot, and mix it with the rest of the ingredients. Put into a large saucepan and bring almost to the boil. Strain and float more slices of thinly sliced orange on the top.

ELDERBERRY PUNCH

1 PINT ELDERBERRY WINE (*see page* 44), 2 ORANGES,
THINLY SLICED, 2 LEMONS, THINLY SLICED,
6 CLOVES, 1 HEAPED TEASPOON CINNAMON,
½ lb GRANULATED SUGAR

Place all into a saucepan and very slowly bring *almost* to boiling point. Stir well till sugar has dissolved. Strain and serve at once.

❧ *'Erby Townsend was always getting drunk. He could often be seen going from cottage to cottage in the village, calling on his cronies, and having what he called 'sippers' at each, which was really tasting anything that they might have to offer in the way of home-made wine. So by the end of his visiting he was well and truly drunk. The vicar tried hard to get him to stay sober without much success. One Saturday afternoon Erby was staggering home, almost legless, when he happened to meet the reverend gentleman. The vicar said to 'Erby, 'Drunk again Mr Townsend.' 'Erby looked at him with bleery eyes and said 'Ah, so be I vicar.'*

TWO RED ROCKETS

[1]

I PINT RED WINE (*mixed fruit wine recommended*),
I PINT WHITE WINE (*elderflower or meadow sweet*),
I PINT FRESHLY BREWED TEA (*any sort will do*),
I ORANGE, THINLY SLICED, I LEMON, THINLY SLICED,
I LARGE APPLE, THINLY SLICED, I2 OZ DEMERARA
SUGAR, I TEASPOON NUTMEG, I TEASPOON CINNAMON,
I TIN SLICED PEACHES

Put the sugar, spices, strained tea, lemon, orange and apple
into a saucepan. Bring almost to the boil and simmer very
gently till the sugar has dissolved. Add the wines and heat
again. Strain, and tip the tin of sliced peaches on top. Serve
at once.

[2]

I BOTTLE ANY GOOD HOME-MADE RED WINE
(*elderberry or blackberry recommended*), I ROASTED ORANGE,
STUCK WITH A DOZEN CLOVES, $\frac{1}{2}$ lb DEMERARA
SUGAR, 6 TABLESPOONS OF RUM

Put the orange stuck with cloves into a hot oven for about half
an hour. Put the wine into a saucepan and bring almost to the
boil. Add the rum and sugar and stir, then float the orange on
the top. Serve at once.

LIQUEURS

BLACKCURRANT GIN &
CHERRY GIN

$\frac{1}{2}$ lb BLACKCURRANTS, CASTOR SUGAR,
I PINT OF GIN

Pick the stalks from the berries and place them in a mixing
bowl and crush the fruit with a large wooden spoon. Tip fruit
and juice into a kilner jar and add the gin. Screw the bottle
down and leave for about eight weeks. Then strain the liquor
into a bowl and add six ounces of sugar to each pint of juice.
Cover and leave for three days, stirring a couple of times a day
to make sure that all the sugar has dissolved. Strain and bottle
the blackcurrant gin. Keep for four months before drinking.
CHERRY GIN is made by the same method as blackcurrant
gin. Some people don't take the stalks off the cherries. Keep
the gin-soaked cherries after straining and serve them with
before-dinner drinks.

CHERRY BRANDY

1 lb FIRM RIPE CHERRIES, ¾ lb CASTER SUGAR,
6 BLANCHED ALMONDS, 1 PINT BRANDY

Remove the stalks and roll the cherries in a clean tea towel. Then put alternate layers of cherries and sugar into a kilner jar. Screw down and shake a couple of times a day for four days. Then add the brandy and the blanched almonds. Screw down again and leave for at least three months before straining, first through muslin and then through filter paper. Bottle and try to keep till Christmas. Use the brandy-soaked cherries in a trifle.

DAMSON GIN

1 lb DAMSONS, 1 PINT GIN, $\frac{1}{2}$ lb SUGAR, $\frac{1}{4}$ PINT SHERRY

Free the fruit from stalks and wipe them clean by rolling them in a tea towel. Pierce every damson with a darning needle and drop into a large jar. Tip in gin, sugar and sherry over the damsons. Tie down with kitchen foil but gently shake the jar once a day for a couple of weeks. Leave for a further three months before straining off into jars. Finally filter through filter papers before drinking. (Wine filter papers can be bought in packets of a hundred from chemists.)

❧ *What's drinking?*
A mere pause from thinking.

LORD BYRON (1788–1824)

MARROW RUM

1 LARGE FIRM HARVESTED MARROW (*don't use young green ones*), DEMERARA SUGAR, 1 lb RAISINS, $\frac{1}{2}$ oz DRIED YEAST

Cut the top off your marrow and scoop out all the seeds and soft pith. Fill the hole to the top with demerara sugar. Mix up the yeast with a tablespoon of warm water, and top the sugar up with this mixture. Put the marrow's 'lid' back on: either tie it on lengthways or stick it on with sellotape. Stand the marrow upright in a large jug. Cover it with a cloth and keep it in a warm room. When the yeast has stopped working, strain off the liquid from the marrow and measure it. Add one pound of chopped raisins to each gallon of liquid. Put all into your demijohn for a week. Strain and bottle.

ORANGE GIN & ORANGE WHISKY

3 ORANGES, 2 LEMONS, I PINT GIN, I½ lb SUGAR

Grate the rinds of the oranges and lemons into a bowl and then add the juice from them. Add the gin and the sugar and stir all together until the sugar has dissolved. Cover and leave for three weeks, stirring every day. Then strain and bottle off. The longer you can keep this, the better it will be.

ORANGE WHISKY can be made in much the same way just by substituting whisky for gin.

❧ *Once you have opened a bottle of country wine, there is no need to use it all at once. Tightly corked it will keep indefinitely, so you can take a swig when you like.*

RASPBERRY BRANDY

1 lb RASPBERRIES, 1 PINT BRANDY, 1 lb CASTER
SUGAR, PINCH OF CINNAMON

Hull the fruit and put in a large jar. Pour over it the brandy
and sugar and cinnamon. Cover and leave to steep in this for
a month. Strain and bottle; it should be ready to drink in six
months.

RASPBERRY GIN

I tried this last year for the first time, there being a glut of
raspberries. Drunk at Christmas time, it made a lovely change
from sloe gin or any of the more popular drinks.

2 lb RASPBERRIES, 1 PINT GIN, 1 lb SUGAR

Hull the fruit and put it into a stone jar together with the
sugar and gin. Cover with kitchen foil. Stir for three or four
days running to make sure that all the sugar has dissolved.
Leave for six months, after which the gin will be a lovely
colour and very clear. Strain off fruit (which can be used in
a trifle) and bottle. Super!

❧ Silas Moore was the village carter round these parts, journeying between Oxford and all the villages that lay along the way, and he'd fetch and carry most anything folk wanted. Used to go shopping for the ladies too, he'd buy combs and corsets, flannelette nightgowns and calico knickers, he didn't mind what it was, he took it all in his stride.

But he had one fault, he used to get dead drunk. Regular on a Wednesday when he came home from Oxford Market he'd call at the cottages delivering the goods he'd bought for the housewives and all of them used to ask him to take a drop of wine and before he got to his own village he was as tight as a tic. But before he reached home he used to pull up at a quiet spot called Bell Bridge and sleep it off.

Well, one day some of the local farm labourers who were working in a nearby field thought they'd play a trick on the old carrier, and as soon as he dropped off to sleep they un-hitched his horses and turned them out into a field. Then one of the men sat under the cart and waited for old Silas to wake up.

About five o'clock that afternoon Silas woke. He set bolt upright in the cart, then looked round fuddled-like, a-scratching his head, wondering where he was. Then he said to himself 'Silas Moore, I reckons you be dead, well if it's I, that is, but if it ent I, who be I?'

Then he noticed that his horses were gone and said 'Well, if it is I, I've lost two hosses, but if it ent I, I've found a cart!'

RASPBERRY LIQUEUR

1 lb RASPBERRIES, 1 lb SUGAR, 1 PINT GIN,
1 PINT WATER

Pick over the fruit and put into a kilner jar along with the gin.
Cover and leave in a warm place for two or three days. Put
the sugar and water together in a saucepan and boil up
together, skimming off any scum as it forms. Leave to get cold.
Strain the raspberries and add the cold liquid to the juice.
Bottle off.

*A neighbour of mine used to come in and sample 'a drop o wine'
now and then. After a couple of glasses she'd get quite tiddly. One day
she said 'Missus, that sloe wine o' yourn makes I all of a twitter,
that it do.'*

TWO SLOE GINS

[1]

1 lb SLOES, 6 OZ CASTER SUGAR, I PINT GIN

Pick all the stalks from the fruit. Prick each sloe several times with a large darning needle before dropping them into a kilner-type jar. Add the sugar and screw the jar down. Shake the jar daily for a couple of weeks. Then add the gin and screw down again and leave for three months. Strain, bottle, and drink when the fancy takes you.

[2]

1½ lb SLOES, 1½ lb GRANULATED SUGAR, 1½ PINTS GIN

Pick the stalks from the fruit and put them in a large jar – an old sweet jar is ideal. Add the sugar and the gin and screw down. Shake the jar daily for about three weeks, until the sugar has all dissolved. Leave for about three months before straining, but the longer this is left the better. By using more sugar a thicker, richer drink is produced.

✤ *Did you know that the Pilgrim Fathers took sloe gin with them on their long, hazardous journey to the New World? It was used medicinally, of course, and was supposed to combat scurvy and the other ailments that were likely to befall them.*

THE LOVE POTION

A spinster lady in a village near where we lived as children was called Mary Ellen Brown. Most of her life had been taken up by looking after her ailing mother and father. But after they died she surprised everyone by opening up a little shop in the front room of her house, where she sold the most delicious assortment of home-made sweets, and the wonderful smell that floated across the green when she was 'boiling up' tickled the nostrils of everyone who happened by.

She also made a goodly supply of rhubarb wine every year and some folks reckoned that she had got some stored away that was ten years old. Rhubarb was all that grew in her overgrown garden, which, folk said, looked like a forest of elephants' ears. The wine, Mary Ellen said, was 'for medical purposes only'. Occasionally she would give a bottle of it away, and those who had the privilege of sampling it said that it was some very potent stuff.

On this particularly cold frosty January night, bachelor George Stokes had stopped to chatter with some of his cronies after the parish tea festivities before cycling home, and when he did reach the village he noticed the light was still on in Mary Ellen's home. Coo, he thought, what wouldn't I give for a drop of Mary Ellen's celebrated rhubarb wine to warm me up! While these thoughts were running through his head, the light in the cottage went out and the village street seemed darker and colder than ever.

Whether it was the excitement of the evening, or the fact that Sam Finch had sent George on his way with a glass of his special parsnip wine, but we shall probably never know what made George act the way he did. He had heard that the famous rhubarb wine was kept locked up in the shed, next to the cottage. So he propped his bicycle up against Mary Ellen's gate and crept quietly into the yard. After a good deal of pushing and pulling, shoving and grunting, he managed to remove a couple of the wooden panels from the side of the shed. He squeezed himself through the opening and his eyes popped out like chapel hat pegs. There, neatly laid on their sides, were dozens and dozens of bottles, filled with the pale pink nectar. He struck a match, all the bottles were labelled and dated. He went along the neat rows striking match after match, reading as he went – 1921, 1920, 1919. 'Ah,' he exclaimed, 'This is the one, made May 1918, bottled July 1918, I'll try this one for a start,' George muttered to himself. He pulled the cork, took a sniff, and then a long, long drink. This thought George Stokes, is the wine of the gods, wine of a long-forgotten summer, heady and sweet.

By mid-morning the next day it was all round the village that George Stokes had spent the night with Mary Ellen Brown. At five o'clock that morning postman Tempest had seen George's bicycle propped up outside Mary Ellen's cottage and it was still there at midday when the baker went by.

'I don't believe it,' the postman's wife said when her husband told her the news. 'Mary Ellen wouldn't do such a thing.'

'Well, why don't you go down to her shop and buy yerself two penneth of clove sweets,' her husband retorted. 'You will see for yerself then.'

'You'd a thought he'd a had the decency to have took his bicycle round the back, out of the way, wouldn't you?' Bertha Botherum the village gossip said. 'Downright disgraceful I calls it,' she went on, 'And at 'er age too, 'er's sixty if 'er's a day.'

Poor Mary Ellen knew nothing about these tales that were flashing round the village like wildfire. Mind you, she had had two or three customers in for sweets that morning who had seemed highly amused about something. And then there was Mrs Crook, usually so friendly and chattery, but on this morning she had a job to even pass the time of day with Mary Ellen. Mrs Crook always came in on a Wednesday morning to buy her weekly half pound of humbugs which she took to her old mother who lived at Aston, and she fair flounced out of the shop with a very curt 'good-morning'. Then there was Jimmy Drake, he had actually winked at Mary Ellen as he went out.

About three o'clock that afternoon she went to the shed to get a few dry logs for the fire, and she noticed that some of the wooden panels had been forced from the side of it. 'Now I wonder who did that,' she thought. 'Best to unlock the door first to see if anything has been stolen, then I must see if I can fix the wood back where it belongs.'

Mary Ellen unlocked the door and pushed it open, then she let out a terrific scream, there, sprawled on the floor, surrounded by empty wine bottles, his mouth wide open, was George Stokes, and he looked as if he was dead.

Postman Tempest who was just going past on his afternoon rounds, heard the screaming, he threw his bicycle on the grass verge and went running up the path to see what on earth was happening. He found Mary Ellen bending over the prostrate form of George Stokes, she was almost hysterical, crying over and over again, 'He's dead, he's dead.'

The postman bent down and touched the body, and sniffed, 'He's dead all right, Miss, dead drunk that's all. Come on,' he said. 'We had best get him into the house.'

Mary Ellen and George were married a few weeks later on St Valentine's Day, and they enjoyed several years of happy married bliss.

The next year there was a special fête in the village to raise money for the church funds, so Mary Ellen and George offered some of the *bottles of wine to be used in a raffle. My blessed, didn't those raffle tickets sell well, when folk knew that they stood a chance of winning a bottle of that wine. You see, that wine was a sort of symbol of re-vitalizing, giving the men back their youth and all that, at least that is what some people thought, and it was that wine that was blamed for a lot of things that followed in the villages around durng the next year. Forty-year-old Mrs Snaith had twins, fifteen yʹırs after her last was born. Harry Patson went off with a housemaid from Lord B's estate, leaving his wife and seven children to fend for themselves, and there were ten weddings in as many months. And they reckons that all these parties had won bottles of Mary Ellen's wine.*

INDEX